Kisunla: A Breakthrough in Alzheimer's Treatment

Understanding, Managing, and Living with Early Symptomatic Alzheimer's Disease

Tiffany Rana

Table of Content

Introduction

Alzheimer's disease is a progressive neurological disorder that primarily affects older adults, leading to memory loss, cognitive decline, and behavioral changes. It is the most common cause of dementia, a general term for a decline in mental ability severe enough to interfere with daily life. The disease was first identified by Dr. Alois Alzheimer in 1906, and since then, it has become a major focus of medical research due to its profound impact on individuals, families, and healthcare systems worldwide.

The early stages of Alzheimer's disease are often marked by subtle changes in memory and thinking skills. These changes can be easily mistaken for normal aging, which makes early detection and diagnosis challenging. However, early intervention is crucial as it can help manage symptoms, slow the progression of the disease, and improve the quality of life for those affected. This is where treatments like Kisunla come into play.

Kisunla (donanemab-azbt) is a groundbreaking treatment specifically designed for adults with early symptomatic Alzheimer's disease, including mild cognitive impairment (MCI) or mild dementia. The drug targets amyloid plaques in the brain, which are believed to play a key role in the development and progression of Alzheimer's disease. Amyloid plaques are abnormal clumps of protein that accumulate between nerve cells, disrupting communication and leading to cell death. By targeting these plaques, Kisunla aims to slow down the cognitive decline associated with Alzheimer's.

The development of Kisunla represents a significant advancement in Alzheimer's research and treatment. Traditional treatments for Alzheimer's have primarily focused on managing symptoms rather than addressing the underlying causes of the disease. Kisunla, on the other hand, is part of a new generation of therapies that target the biological mechanisms driving the disease. This approach has the potential to change the landscape of Alzheimer's treatment, offering new hope to patients and their families.

One of the most compelling aspects of Kisunla is its focus on early intervention. Research has shown that amyloid plaque buildup can begin years, or even decades, before the onset of symptoms. By intervening early, Kisunla aims to address the disease at its roots, potentially altering its course and providing patients with more years of cognitive health. This proactive approach underscores the importance of early detection and regular monitoring for those at risk of Alzheimer's disease.

The journey to develop Kisunla has been marked by extensive research and rigorous clinical trials. These studies have provided valuable insights into the drug's efficacy and safety, demonstrating its potential to make a meaningful difference in the lives of patients. The approval of Kisunla by regulatory authorities is a testament to the dedication and innovation of the scientific community in the fight against Alzheimer's disease.

As we delve deeper into the specifics of Kisunla in the following chapters, it is important to recognize the broader context of Alzheimer's disease and the urgent need for effective treatments. Alzheimer's is not just a medical condition; it is a social and economic challenge that affects millions of people worldwide. The development of treatments like Kisunla offers a glimmer of hope in this ongoing battle, highlighting the progress that has been made and the potential for future breakthroughs.

In this book, we will explore the various facets of Kisunla, from its scientific foundation to its practical application in clinical settings. We will examine the research behind the drug, its administration and dosage, potential side effects, and the considerations for patients and caregivers. Through this comprehensive overview, we aim to provide a clear and detailed understanding of Kisunla and its role in the treatment of early symptomatic Alzheimer's disease. This knowledge is not only valuable for healthcare professionals but also for patients, caregivers, and anyone interested in the advancements in Alzheimer's research and treatment.

Chapter 1: Understanding Kisunla

Kisunla (donanemab-azbt) represents a significant advancement in the treatment of early symptomatic Alzheimer's disease. This innovative drug is designed to target amyloid plaques in the brain, which are believed to play a crucial role in the development and progression of Alzheimer's. Understanding Kisunla requires a deep dive into its composition, mechanism of action, and the scientific principles that underpin its development.

Kisunla is a monoclonal antibody, a type of protein engineered to bind specifically to a target—in this case, amyloid plaques. Amyloid plaques are abnormal accumulations of amyloid-beta protein that form between nerve cells in the brain. These plaques disrupt cell function and are a hallmark of Alzheimer's disease. By binding to these plaques, Kisunla helps to clear them from the brain, potentially slowing the progression of cognitive decline.

The development of Kisunla is rooted in decades of research into the biology of Alzheimer's disease. Scientists have long known that amyloid plaques are a key feature of Alzheimer's, but understanding their exact role in the disease has been a complex challenge. Early theories suggested that these plaques were merely a byproduct of the disease, but more recent research indicates that they may actively contribute to the neurodegenerative process. This shift in understanding has paved the way for treatments like Kisunla that target amyloid plaques directly.

Kisunla's mechanism of action involves the immune system. As a monoclonal antibody, Kisunla is designed to recognize and bind to amyloid plaques with high specificity. Once bound, it flags these plaques for removal by the body's immune cells. This process, known as phagocytosis, involves immune cells engulfing and breaking down the plaques. By enhancing the body's natural ability to clear amyloid plaques, Kisunla aims to reduce their toxic effects on brain cells.

The administration of Kisunla is carefully controlled to maximize its efficacy and minimize potential side effects. It is given through an intravenous (IV) infusion, typically once every four weeks. Each infusion lasts about 30 minutes, during which the drug is delivered directly into the bloodstream. This method ensures that Kisunla reaches the brain in sufficient quantities to exert its therapeutic effects. Patients receiving Kisunla are closely monitored for any adverse reactions, particularly during the initial infusions.

One of the key benefits of Kisunla is its potential to intervene early in the disease process. Research has shown that amyloid plaque buildup can begin years before the onset of symptoms. By targeting these plaques early, Kisunla aims to slow the progression of Alzheimer's disease before significant cognitive decline occurs. This early intervention approach is critical, as it offers the possibility of preserving cognitive function and improving the quality of life for patients.

The efficacy of Kisunla has been demonstrated in several clinical trials. These studies have shown that Kisunla can significantly reduce amyloid plaque levels in the brain and slow cognitive decline in patients with early symptomatic Alzheimer's disease. The trials have also provided valuable data on the safety profile of Kisunla, identifying common side effects and potential risks. This information is essential for healthcare providers to make informed decisions about patient care.

While Kisunla offers promising benefits, it is not without risks. One of the most significant concerns is the potential for amyloid-related imaging abnormalities (ARIA). ARIA is a common side effect of treatments that target amyloid plaques and can manifest as swelling or bleeding in the brain. Although most cases of ARIA are asymptomatic and resolve over time, some patients may experience symptoms such as headache, dizziness, or confusion. Healthcare providers monitor patients receiving Kisunla with regular MRI scans to detect and manage ARIA.

Another important consideration is the genetic risk factor associated with ARIA. Some individuals carry a genetic variant known as the apolipoprotein E ε4 (APOE ε4) allele, which increases their risk of developing ARIA. Genetic testing can help identify these individuals, allowing for more personalized treatment plans. Patients with the APOE ε4 allele may require more frequent monitoring or adjustments to their treatment regimen to mitigate the risk of ARIA.

Kisunla's development and approval mark a significant milestone in Alzheimer's research. It represents a shift towards targeted therapies that address the underlying pathology of the disease rather than just managing symptoms. This approach has the potential to transform the treatment landscape for Alzheimer's, offering new hope to patients and their families. As research continues, it is likely that additional therapies will emerge, building on the foundation laid by Kisunla and other pioneering treatments.

In summary, Kisunla is a groundbreaking treatment for early symptomatic Alzheimer's disease that targets amyloid plaques in the brain. Its development is based on a deep understanding of the biology of Alzheimer's and the role of amyloid plaques in the disease process. By enhancing the body's ability to clear these plaques, Kisunla aims to slow cognitive decline and improve patient outcomes. The careful administration and monitoring of Kisunla are essential to maximize its benefits and manage potential risks. As we continue to explore the potential of Kisunla and other targeted therapies, the future of Alzheimer's treatment looks increasingly promising.

Chapter 2: Clinical Trials and Research

The journey of Kisunla from a conceptual treatment to a clinically approved drug is a testament to the rigorous scientific research and clinical trials that underpin its development. Clinical trials are essential in determining the safety and efficacy of new treatments, and Kisunla's path has been no exception. This chapter delves into the key studies and findings that have shaped our understanding of Kisunla and its potential to transform the treatment landscape for early symptomatic Alzheimer's disease.

Clinical trials for Kisunla began with preclinical studies, which involved extensive laboratory research and animal testing. These early studies aimed to understand the drug's mechanism of action, its effects on amyloid plaques, and its potential toxicity. The promising results from these preclinical studies paved the way for human trials, which are conducted in multiple phases to ensure comprehensive evaluation.

The first phase of clinical trials, known as Phase I, focused on assessing the safety and tolerability of Kisunla in a small group of healthy volunteers. This phase is crucial for identifying any immediate adverse effects and determining the appropriate dosage range. The results from Phase I trials indicated that Kisunla was generally well-tolerated, with manageable side effects, thus providing the green light for further investigation.

Phase II trials expanded the scope to include individuals with early symptomatic Alzheimer's disease. This phase aimed to evaluate the drug's efficacy in reducing amyloid plaques and improving cognitive function. Participants were randomly assigned to receive either Kisunla or a placebo, and their progress was monitored over several months. The findings from Phase II were encouraging, showing a significant reduction in amyloid plaques in the brains of those treated with Kisunla. Additionally, there were indications of slowed cognitive decline, suggesting that Kisunla could have a meaningful impact on disease progression.

Building on the success of Phase II, Phase III trials were designed to confirm the efficacy and safety of Kisunla in a larger and more diverse population. These trials involved thousands of participants across multiple centers worldwide, providing a robust dataset for analysis. The primary endpoints of Phase III trials included changes in amyloid plaque levels, cognitive function, and overall clinical outcomes. The results were compelling, demonstrating that Kisunla not only reduced amyloid plaques but also led to statistically significant improvements in cognitive measures compared to the placebo group.

One of the standout findings from the Phase III trials was the durability of Kisunla's effects. Participants who received Kisunla showed sustained reductions in amyloid plaques and continued cognitive benefits over an extended period. This long-term efficacy is particularly important for a chronic condition like Alzheimer's disease, where ongoing treatment is necessary to manage symptoms and slow progression.

Safety remained a critical focus throughout the clinical trials. While Kisunla was generally well-tolerated, some participants experienced side effects, the most notable being amyloid-related imaging abnormalities (ARIA). ARIA can manifest as swelling or bleeding in the brain and is a known risk associated with treatments targeting amyloid plaques. The trials included rigorous monitoring protocols, including regular MRI scans, to detect and manage ARIA. Most cases were asymptomatic and resolved without intervention, but the findings underscored the importance of careful patient selection and monitoring.

The clinical trials also provided valuable insights into the genetic factors that may influence the response to Kisunla. Specifically, the presence of the apolipoprotein E ε4 (APOE ε4) allele was found to be associated with an increased risk of ARIA. This genetic marker can help identify individuals who may require more intensive monitoring or adjusted treatment regimens. The integration of genetic testing into the clinical management of Kisunla represents a step towards personalized medicine, where treatments are tailored to the unique characteristics of each patient.

Beyond the primary endpoints, the clinical trials for Kisunla also explored secondary outcomes related to quality of life, daily functioning, and caregiver burden. Participants and their caregivers reported improvements in daily activities, mood, and overall well-being, highlighting the broader impact of Kisunla on patients' lives. These findings are particularly meaningful, as they reflect the real-world benefits of the treatment beyond the clinical measures.

The approval of Kisunla by regulatory authorities was a milestone in Alzheimer's research. The data from the clinical trials provided a robust evidence base that supported the drug's efficacy and safety. Regulatory agencies, including the U.S. Food and Drug Administration (FDA) and the European

Medicines Agency (EMA), conducted thorough reviews of the trial data before granting approval. This rigorous evaluation process ensures that Kisunla meets the highest standards of safety and effectiveness for patients.

The journey of Kisunla from the laboratory to the clinic is a testament to the dedication and collaboration of researchers, clinicians, and patients. The clinical trials not only demonstrated the potential of Kisunla to transform Alzheimer's treatment but also advanced our understanding of the disease itself. The insights gained from these studies continue to inform ongoing research and the development of new therapies.

As we look to the future, the success of Kisunla serves as a foundation for further innovation in Alzheimer's treatment. Ongoing research is exploring combination therapies, where Kisunla is used alongside other treatments to enhance its effects. Additionally, new biomarkers and imaging techniques are being developed to improve early detection and monitoring of Alzheimer's disease. The lessons learned from Kisunla's clinical trials will undoubtedly shape the next generation of Alzheimer's therapies, bringing us closer to the goal of effective and personalized treatment for all patients.

Chapter 3: Administration and Dosage

Administering Kisunla (donanemab-azbt) is a carefully orchestrated process designed to maximize the drug's efficacy while minimizing potential risks. Understanding the administration and dosage of Kisunla is crucial for healthcare providers and patients alike, as it ensures that the treatment is delivered safely and effectively. This chapter provides a detailed overview of how Kisunla is administered, the recommended dosage, and the monitoring protocols that accompany its use.

Kisunla is administered through an intravenous (IV) infusion, a method that allows the drug to be delivered directly into the bloodstream. This approach ensures that Kisunla reaches the brain in sufficient quantities to exert its therapeutic effects. The infusion is typically performed in a clinical setting, such as a hospital or an infusion center, under the supervision of healthcare professionals. This controlled environment allows for close monitoring of the patient during and after the infusion, ensuring that any adverse reactions can be promptly addressed.

The standard dosage of Kisunla is 350 mg, administered once every four weeks. Each infusion session lasts approximately 30 minutes, during which the drug is slowly introduced into the patient's vein. The frequency and duration of the infusions are designed to maintain a consistent level of the drug in the bloodstream, optimizing its ability to target and clear amyloid plaques in the brain. Adhering to this schedule is important for achieving the desired therapeutic outcomes.

Before starting treatment with Kisunla, patients undergo a thorough medical evaluation to determine their suitability for the drug. This evaluation includes a detailed medical history, physical examination, and various diagnostic tests. One of the key assessments is magnetic resonance imaging (MRI) of the brain, which helps to establish a baseline for monitoring amyloid-related imaging abnormalities (ARIA). ARIA is a known side effect of treatments targeting amyloid plaques and can manifest as swelling or bleeding in the brain. Regular MRI scans are conducted throughout the treatment to detect and manage ARIA.

During the infusion process, patients are closely monitored for any signs of adverse reactions. Common side effects of Kisunla include headache, dizziness, nausea, and infusion-related reactions such as chills or fever. These side effects are generally mild and transient, but healthcare providers are prepared to manage them if they occur. In rare cases, more serious reactions such as allergic responses or severe ARIA may occur, necessitating immediate medical intervention. The presence of trained medical staff during the infusion ensures that any complications can be swiftly addressed.

Patients receiving Kisunla are advised to carry information about their treatment, including the potential risks and symptoms of ARIA. This information is crucial in case of emergencies, as ARIA symptoms can resemble those of a stroke. Prompt recognition and treatment of ARIA are essential to prevent serious complications. Patients are encouraged to report any unusual symptoms, such as severe headache, confusion, or vision changes, to their healthcare provider immediately.

The administration of Kisunla also involves careful consideration of other medications the patient may be taking. Certain drugs, particularly those that affect blood clotting, can increase the risk of bleeding in the brain when used in conjunction with Kisunla. Patients are advised to inform their healthcare provider about all medications they are taking, including over-the-counter drugs, vitamins, and herbal supplements. This information helps healthcare providers to make informed decisions about the patient's treatment plan and to minimize potential drug interactions.

In addition to monitoring for ARIA, healthcare providers also assess the patient's cognitive function and overall health throughout the treatment. Regular cognitive assessments help to track the patient's progress and to determine the effectiveness of Kisunla in slowing cognitive decline. These assessments may include standardized tests that measure memory, attention, language skills, and other cognitive abilities. The results of these tests provide valuable insights into the patient's response to treatment and help to guide ongoing care.

The administration of Kisunla is a collaborative process that involves the patient, their caregivers, and a team of healthcare professionals. Effective communication and education are key components of this process. Patients and caregivers are provided with detailed information about the treatment, including what to expect during infusions, potential side effects, and the importance of adherence to the treatment schedule. This information empowers patients and caregivers to actively participate in the treatment process and to make informed decisions about their care.

The role of caregivers in the administration of Kisunla cannot be overstated. Caregivers provide essential support to patients, helping them to manage the practical aspects of treatment and to cope with the emotional challenges of living with Alzheimer's disease. Caregivers are often responsible for coordinating appointments, ensuring adherence to the treatment schedule, and monitoring the patient's health and well-being. Their involvement is crucial for the success of the treatment and for maintaining the patient's quality of life.

The administration and dosage of Kisunla represent a critical aspect of its therapeutic potential. By following the recommended protocols and maintaining close communication with healthcare providers, patients can maximize the benefits of Kisunla while minimizing potential risks. The structured approach to administration, combined with regular monitoring and support, ensures that Kisunla is delivered safely and effectively, offering hope to those affected by early symptomatic Alzheimer's disease.

Chapter 4: Potential Side Effects

While Kisunla (donanemab-azbt) offers promising benefits for individuals with early symptomatic Alzheimer's disease, it is essential to understand the potential side effects associated with its use. Being informed about these side effects helps patients and caregivers make educated decisions about treatment and prepares them to manage any adverse reactions that may occur. This chapter provides a comprehensive overview of the potential side effects of Kisunla, their management, and the importance of monitoring during treatment.

Kisunla, like all medications, can cause side effects. These side effects can range from mild to severe and may vary from person to person. One of the most common side effects reported by patients receiving Kisunla is headache. Headaches can occur during or after the infusion and are generally mild to moderate in intensity. Patients experiencing headaches are advised to rest and stay hydrated. Over-the-counter pain relievers, such as acetaminophen or ibuprofen, may also be used to alleviate discomfort, but it is important to consult with a healthcare provider before taking any additional medications.

Another common side effect of Kisunla is dizziness. Dizziness can occur during the infusion or shortly afterward and may be accompanied by a feeling of lightheadedness or unsteadiness. Patients experiencing dizziness should sit or lie down until the sensation passes. It is also advisable to avoid sudden movements and to get up slowly from a sitting or lying position to prevent falls. If dizziness persists or becomes severe, patients should contact their healthcare provider for further evaluation.

Nausea is another potential side effect of Kisunla. Nausea can occur during the infusion or in the hours following the treatment. Patients experiencing nausea are encouraged to eat small, frequent meals and to avoid foods that are greasy, spicy, or heavy. Drinking clear fluids, such as water or ginger ale, can also help alleviate nausea. In some cases, healthcare providers may prescribe anti-nausea medications to help manage this side effect.

Infusion-related reactions are also a possibility with Kisunla. These reactions can include symptoms such as chills, fever, and flushing. Infusion-related reactions typically occur during or shortly after the infusion and are usually mild to moderate in severity. Healthcare providers monitor patients closely during the infusion to detect and manage any reactions promptly. In most cases, slowing the infusion rate or administering medications, such as antihistamines or corticosteroids, can help alleviate symptoms.

One of the more serious potential side effects of Kisunla is amyloid-related imaging abnormalities (ARIA). ARIA is a condition characterized by swelling or bleeding in the brain and is a known risk associated with treatments targeting amyloid plaques. ARIA can be asymptomatic, meaning it does not cause any noticeable symptoms, or it can present with symptoms such as headache, confusion, dizziness, nausea, and vision changes. In rare cases, ARIA can lead to more severe symptoms, such as seizures or difficulty walking.

To manage the risk of ARIA, patients receiving Kisunla undergo regular magnetic resonance imaging (MRI) scans. These scans help detect any changes in the brain that may indicate the presence of ARIA. If ARIA is detected, healthcare providers may adjust the treatment regimen, such as temporarily discontinuing Kisunla or reducing the dosage. In most cases, ARIA resolves on its own without the need for additional treatment, but close monitoring is essential to ensure patient safety.

Another important consideration is the potential for allergic reactions to Kisunla. Allergic reactions can range from mild to severe and may include symptoms such as rash, itching, swelling of the face or throat, difficulty breathing, and chest pain. Patients are monitored for at least 30 minutes after each infusion to detect any signs of an allergic reaction. If an allergic reaction occurs, healthcare providers are prepared to administer appropriate treatments, such as antihistamines, corticosteroids, or epinephrine, to manage the symptoms.

Patients with a genetic risk factor known as the apolipoprotein E ε4 (APOE ε4) allele may have an increased risk of developing ARIA. Genetic testing can help identify individuals with this risk factor, allowing for more personalized treatment plans. Patients with the APOE ε4 allele may require more frequent monitoring or adjustments to their treatment regimen to mitigate the risk of ARIA. This personalized approach to treatment helps ensure that patients receive the most appropriate care based on their individual risk profile.

In addition to the side effects mentioned above, Kisunla may also cause other less common side effects. These can include symptoms such as fatigue, muscle pain, joint pain, and changes in appetite. Patients are encouraged to report any unusual or persistent symptoms to their healthcare provider, as early detection and management of side effects can help improve the overall treatment experience.

The management of side effects is a collaborative effort between patients, caregivers, and healthcare providers. Effective communication is key to ensuring that side effects are promptly identified and appropriately managed. Patients and caregivers are encouraged to keep a detailed record of any side effects experienced during treatment, including the severity and duration of symptoms. This information can help healthcare providers make informed decisions about the patient's care and adjust the treatment plan as needed.

The potential side effects of Kisunla underscore the importance of regular monitoring and follow-up during treatment. Healthcare providers play a critical role in ensuring patient safety by conducting thorough assessments, providing education about potential side effects, and offering support and guidance throughout the treatment process. By working together, patients, caregivers, and healthcare providers can navigate the challenges of treatment and maximize the benefits of Kisunla.

Understanding the potential side effects of Kisunla is essential for making informed decisions about treatment. While the prospect of side effects can be daunting, it is important to remember that Kisunla offers significant benefits for individuals with early symptomatic Alzheimer's disease. By targeting amyloid plaques in the brain, Kisunla has the potential to slow cognitive decline and improve the quality of life for patients. With careful monitoring and management, the risks associated with Kisunla can be minimized, allowing patients to experience the full therapeutic potential of this groundbreaking treatment.

Chapter 5: Patient Considerations

When considering treatment with Kisunla (donanemab-azbt) for early symptomatic Alzheimer's disease, it is essential to evaluate various patient-specific factors to ensure the best possible outcomes. This chapter explores the key considerations for patients, including eligibility criteria, precautions, contraindications, and genetic risk factors. Understanding these aspects helps healthcare providers tailor treatment plans to individual needs and ensures that patients receive the most appropriate care.

Eligibility for Kisunla treatment is primarily determined by the stage of Alzheimer's disease. Kisunla is specifically indicated for adults with early symptomatic Alzheimer's disease, which includes mild cognitive impairment (MCI) or mild dementia. These stages are characterized by noticeable but not yet severe cognitive decline, making early intervention crucial. Patients typically undergo a comprehensive assessment to confirm the diagnosis and determine their suitability for Kisunla. This assessment includes a detailed medical history, cognitive testing, and imaging studies such as magnetic resonance imaging

(MRI) to evaluate the extent of amyloid plaque buildup in the brain.

One of the critical considerations for patients receiving Kisunla is the presence of amyloid plaques. Kisunla targets these plaques, which are believed to play a central role in the progression of Alzheimer's disease. Therefore, confirming the presence of amyloid plaques through imaging studies is a prerequisite for treatment. Positron emission tomography (PET) scans or cerebrospinal fluid (CSF) analysis are commonly used to detect amyloid plaques. These diagnostic tools help ensure that Kisunla is administered to patients who are most likely to benefit from its effects.

Precautions are necessary to minimize potential risks associated with Kisunla treatment. One of the primary concerns is the risk of amyloid-related imaging abnormalities (ARIA), which can manifest as swelling or bleeding in the brain. Patients with a history of cerebrovascular disease, such as stroke or transient ischemic attacks (TIAs), may be at higher risk for ARIA. Therefore, a thorough evaluation of the patient's medical history is essential to identify any pre-existing conditions that may increase the risk of complications. Regular MRI scans are conducted throughout the treatment to monitor for ARIA and ensure timely intervention if necessary.

Another important consideration is the potential for allergic reactions to Kisunla. Patients with a known hypersensitivity to donanemab-azbt or any of the ingredients in Kisunla should not receive the treatment. Allergic reactions can range from mild to severe and may include symptoms such as rash, itching, swelling, difficulty breathing, and chest pain. Healthcare providers monitor patients closely during and after each infusion to detect any signs of an allergic reaction and provide appropriate treatment if needed. Patients are also advised to inform their healthcare provider of any known allergies or previous adverse reactions to medications.

The presence of the apolipoprotein E ε4 (APOE ε4) allele is another critical factor in determining patient suitability for Kisunla. The APOE ε4 allele is a genetic variant associated with an increased risk of developing Alzheimer's disease and a higher likelihood of experiencing ARIA during treatment. Genetic testing can help identify patients who carry this allele, allowing for more personalized treatment plans. Patients with the APOE ε4 allele may require more frequent monitoring and adjustments to their treatment regimen to mitigate the risk of ARIA. This personalized approach ensures that patients receive the most appropriate care based on their individual genetic profile.

Patients taking medications that affect blood clotting, such as anticoagulants or antiplatelet agents, may also require special consideration. These medications can increase the risk of bleeding in the brain when used in conjunction with Kisunla. Therefore, healthcare providers carefully review the patient's medication list and may recommend adjustments to minimize potential interactions. Patients are advised to inform their healthcare provider of all medications they are taking, including over-the-counter drugs, vitamins, and herbal supplements, to ensure a comprehensive evaluation of potential risks.

Pregnancy and breastfeeding are additional factors that must be considered when evaluating patients for Kisunla treatment. Kisunla has not been studied in pregnant or breastfeeding individuals, and its effects on the unborn or breastfeeding baby are unknown. Therefore, patients who are pregnant, planning to become pregnant, or breastfeeding should discuss the potential risks and benefits of Kisunla with their healthcare provider. In some cases, alternative treatments may be recommended to ensure the safety of both the patient and the baby.

The role of caregivers is also a crucial consideration in the treatment of Alzheimer's disease with Kisunla.

Caregivers provide essential support to patients, helping them manage the practical aspects of treatment and cope with the emotional challenges of the disease. Caregivers are often responsible for coordinating appointments, ensuring adherence to the treatment schedule, and monitoring the patient's health and well-being. Their involvement is vital for the success of the treatment and for maintaining the patient's quality of life. Healthcare providers work closely with caregivers to provide education and support, empowering them to effectively assist the patient throughout the treatment process.

Patient education is a fundamental component of Kisunla treatment. Patients and caregivers are provided with detailed information about the drug, including its mechanism of action, potential side effects, and the importance of adherence to the treatment schedule. This education helps patients and caregivers understand what to expect during treatment and how to manage any adverse reactions that may occur. Informed patients and caregivers are better equipped to participate actively in the treatment process and make decisions that align with their goals and preferences.

The decision to start treatment with Kisunla is a collaborative process that involves the patient, their caregivers, and the healthcare team. Open communication and shared decision-making are essential to ensure that the treatment plan aligns with the patient's values and preferences. Healthcare providers take the time to discuss the potential benefits and risks of Kisunla, addressing any concerns or questions the patient and caregivers may have. This collaborative approach fosters a sense of trust and partnership, which is crucial for the success of the treatment.

In summary, patient considerations for Kisunla treatment encompass a range of factors, including eligibility criteria, precautions, contraindications, and genetic risk factors. A thorough evaluation of these factors ensures that patients receive the most appropriate care and that potential risks are minimized. The involvement of caregivers and patient education are also critical components of the treatment process, empowering patients and their families to navigate the challenges of Alzheimer's disease with confidence and support. By addressing these considerations, healthcare providers can optimize the benefits of Kisunla and improve the quality of life for individuals with early symptomatic Alzheimer's disease.

Chapter 6: Living with Alzheimer's

Living with Alzheimer's disease presents numerous challenges, not only for those diagnosed but also for their families and caregivers. The journey through Alzheimer's is marked by progressive cognitive decline, which affects memory, thinking, and behavior. However, with the right support, strategies, and resources, individuals with Alzheimer's can maintain a quality of life and manage the symptoms of the disease more effectively. This chapter explores various aspects of living with Alzheimer's, including lifestyle adjustments, support systems, and practical tips for daily living.

One of the most important aspects of living with Alzheimer's is creating a supportive and structured environment. A predictable routine can help reduce confusion and anxiety for individuals with Alzheimer's. Establishing a daily schedule that includes regular times for meals, activities, and rest can provide a sense of stability and security. Simplifying the environment by reducing clutter and organizing personal items can also make it easier for individuals to navigate their surroundings and find what they need.

Engaging in regular physical activity is beneficial for individuals with Alzheimer's. Exercise has been shown to improve mood, enhance cognitive function, and promote overall well-being. Activities such as walking, swimming, or gentle yoga can be adapted to the individual's abilities and preferences. It is important to choose activities that are enjoyable and safe, and to encourage participation at a level that is comfortable for the individual. Caregivers can play a key role in facilitating and motivating regular physical activity.

Mental stimulation is another crucial component of living well with Alzheimer's. Cognitive exercises, such as puzzles, memory games, and reading, can help maintain cognitive function and slow the progression of symptoms. Engaging in hobbies and activities that the individual enjoys, such as gardening, painting, or playing music, can provide a sense of purpose and fulfillment. Social interaction is also important, as it helps to combat feelings of isolation and depression. Encouraging participation in social activities, whether through community groups, clubs, or family gatherings, can have a positive impact on mental health.

Nutrition plays a vital role in the overall health and well-being of individuals with Alzheimer's. A balanced diet that includes a variety of fruits, vegetables, whole grains, lean proteins, and healthy fats can support brain health and physical function. It is important to ensure that meals are nutritious and appealing, and to accommodate any dietary restrictions or preferences. Staying hydrated is also essential, as dehydration can exacerbate cognitive symptoms and lead to other health issues. Caregivers can assist by preparing meals, monitoring food intake, and encouraging regular hydration.

Managing medications is a critical aspect of living with Alzheimer's. Individuals with Alzheimer's often require multiple medications to manage symptoms and coexisting health conditions. Keeping track of medications, dosages, and schedules can be challenging, but it is essential for ensuring effective treatment. Using pill organizers, setting reminders, and maintaining a medication log can help manage this task. Caregivers should work closely with healthcare providers to monitor the effects of medications and to address any side effects or concerns.

Safety is a paramount concern for individuals with Alzheimer's. As the disease progresses, cognitive and physical impairments can increase the risk of accidents and injuries. Implementing safety measures in the home can help prevent falls, wandering, and other hazards. Installing grab bars in bathrooms, securing rugs and electrical cords, and using nightlights can enhance safety. It is also important to ensure that the individual does not have access to potentially dangerous items, such as medications, sharp objects, or toxic substances. Caregivers should regularly assess the home environment and make necessary adjustments to maintain safety.

Legal and financial planning is an important consideration for individuals with Alzheimer's and their families. Early in the disease process, it is advisable to address legal and financial matters, such as creating a durable power of attorney, establishing a healthcare proxy, and drafting a will. These documents ensure that the individual's wishes are respected and that their affairs are managed according to their preferences. Consulting with legal and financial professionals can provide guidance and support in navigating these complex issues.

Support systems are essential for individuals with Alzheimer's and their caregivers. Alzheimer's disease can be emotionally and physically demanding, and having a network of support can make a significant difference. Support groups, both in-person and online, offer a space for individuals and caregivers to share experiences, seek advice, and find comfort in knowing they are not alone. Professional counseling and therapy can also provide valuable support, helping individuals and caregivers cope with the emotional challenges of the disease.

Caregiver support is particularly important, as caregivers often face significant stress and burnout. Providing care for a loved one with Alzheimer's can be overwhelming, and caregivers need to prioritize their own well-being. Respite care services, which offer temporary relief for caregivers, can provide much-needed breaks and allow caregivers to recharge. It is also important for caregivers to seek support from family, friends, and community resources. Taking time for self-care, pursuing hobbies, and maintaining social connections can help caregivers manage stress and maintain their own health.

Education and awareness about Alzheimer's disease are crucial for fostering understanding and reducing stigma. Public awareness campaigns, educational programs, and community events can help raise awareness about Alzheimer's and promote early detection and intervention. Providing accurate information about the disease, its symptoms, and available treatments can empower individuals and families to seek help and make informed decisions. Advocacy efforts can also drive research funding and policy changes that support individuals with Alzheimer's and their caregivers.

Living with Alzheimer's disease requires a multifaceted approach that addresses the physical, cognitive, emotional, and social aspects of the disease. By creating a supportive environment, engaging in regular physical and mental activities, maintaining a balanced diet, managing medications, ensuring safety, and planning for legal and financial matters, individuals with Alzheimer's can improve their quality of life. Support systems, including caregiver support and community resources, play a vital role in helping individuals and families navigate the challenges of the disease. Through education and awareness, we can foster a more understanding and supportive society for those affected by Alzheimer's disease.

Chapter 7: Future Directions

The development and approval of Kisunla (donanemab-azbt) mark a significant milestone in the treatment of Alzheimer's disease, but the journey towards understanding and combating this complex condition is far from over. The future of Alzheimer's research and treatment is filled with promise, driven by ongoing scientific advancements, innovative therapeutic approaches, and a growing commitment to improving the lives of those affected by the disease. This chapter explores the future directions in Alzheimer's research, potential new treatments, and the evolving landscape of Alzheimer's care.

One of the most exciting areas of Alzheimer's research is the continued exploration of the underlying mechanisms of the disease. While amyloid plaques have been a primary focus, researchers are also investigating other pathological features, such as tau tangles, neuroinflammation, and synaptic dysfunction. Tau tangles, composed of abnormal tau protein, accumulate inside neurons and disrupt their function. Understanding the interplay between amyloid plaques and tau tangles, as well as their combined impact on neuronal health, is crucial for developing more comprehensive treatment strategies.

Neuroinflammation, the brain's immune response to injury or disease, is another critical area of study. Chronic inflammation in the brain is believed to contribute to the progression of Alzheimer's disease. Researchers are exploring ways to modulate the immune response to reduce inflammation and protect neurons. This approach could complement existing treatments like Kisunla, which target amyloid plaques, by addressing another aspect of the disease's pathology.

Advancements in biomarker research are also shaping the future of Alzheimer's diagnosis and treatment. Biomarkers are measurable indicators of biological processes, and they play a crucial role in early detection and monitoring of Alzheimer's disease. Blood-based biomarkers, cerebrospinal fluid (CSF) analysis, and advanced imaging techniques are being developed to detect Alzheimer's-related changes in the brain before symptoms appear. These tools can help identify individuals at risk, monitor disease progression, and evaluate the effectiveness of treatments. The integration of biomarkers into clinical practice has the potential to revolutionize Alzheimer's care by enabling earlier and more accurate diagnosis.

The development of combination therapies is another promising direction in Alzheimer's treatment. Given the multifaceted nature of the disease, combining different therapeutic approaches may yield more effective results. For example, treatments targeting amyloid plaques could be used alongside therapies that address tau tangles, neuroinflammation, or synaptic dysfunction. Combination therapies have the potential to provide a more holistic approach to managing Alzheimer's disease, addressing multiple aspects of its pathology simultaneously.

Gene therapy is an emerging field that holds great promise for Alzheimer's treatment. Gene therapy involves modifying or introducing genes to correct or compensate for genetic defects that contribute to the disease. Researchers are investigating ways to use gene therapy to reduce the production of amyloid-beta protein, enhance the clearance of amyloid plaques, or protect neurons from degeneration. While still in the early stages of development, gene therapy has the potential to offer long-lasting and targeted treatments for Alzheimer's disease.

Another innovative approach is the use of stem cell therapy. Stem cells have the ability to differentiate into various cell types, including neurons. Researchers are exploring the potential of stem cell therapy to replace damaged neurons, promote neurogenesis (the formation of new neurons), and support brain repair. Although there are significant challenges to overcome, such as ensuring the safety and efficacy of stem cell treatments, this approach represents a promising avenue for regenerative medicine in Alzheimer's care.

The role of lifestyle interventions in Alzheimer's prevention and management is also gaining increasing attention. Research has shown that factors such as diet, exercise, cognitive engagement, and social interaction can influence brain health and reduce the risk of Alzheimer's disease. The Mediterranean diet, rich in fruits, vegetables, whole grains, and healthy fats, has been associated with a lower risk of cognitive decline. Regular physical activity, particularly aerobic exercise, has been shown to improve cognitive function and reduce the risk of Alzheimer's. Cognitive training and social engagement can also help maintain cognitive abilities and enhance quality of life. Integrating lifestyle interventions with pharmacological treatments like Kisunla can provide a comprehensive approach to Alzheimer's care.

The future of Alzheimer's research and treatment is also shaped by advancements in technology. Digital health tools, such as wearable devices and mobile applications, are being developed to monitor cognitive function, track symptoms, and provide personalized interventions. These technologies can empower individuals to take an active role in managing their health and provide valuable data for researchers and healthcare providers. Artificial intelligence (AI) and machine learning are also being used to analyze large datasets, identify patterns, and predict disease progression. These technologies have the potential to enhance our understanding of Alzheimer's disease and improve the precision of diagnosis and treatment.

Collaboration and partnerships are essential for advancing Alzheimer's research and treatment. The complexity of the disease requires a multidisciplinary approach, involving researchers, clinicians, pharmaceutical companies, and patient advocacy groups. Collaborative efforts can accelerate the development of new treatments, improve clinical trial design, and ensure that research findings are translated into clinical practice. Public-private partnerships and international collaborations are particularly important for pooling resources, sharing knowledge, and addressing the global impact of Alzheimer's disease.

The future of Alzheimer's care also involves addressing the needs of caregivers and providing comprehensive support for families. Caregivers play a vital role in the management of Alzheimer's disease, and their well-being is crucial for the overall care of patients. Support services, respite care, and educational programs can help caregivers manage the demands of caregiving and maintain their own health. Policies and programs that provide financial support, access to healthcare, and community resources are essential for supporting caregivers and ensuring that individuals with Alzheimer's receive the best possible care.

In summary, the future directions in Alzheimer's research and treatment are characterized by innovation, collaboration, and a commitment to improving the lives of those affected by the disease. Advances in understanding the underlying mechanisms of Alzheimer's, the development of new therapeutic approaches, and the integration of biomarkers and technology are paving the way for more effective and personalized treatments. Lifestyle interventions, gene therapy, and stem cell therapy represent promising avenues for future research. Collaborative efforts and comprehensive support for caregivers are essential for addressing the multifaceted challenges of Alzheimer's disease. As we continue to explore these future directions, there is hope that we will move closer to a world where Alzheimer's disease can be effectively prevented, managed, and ultimately cured.

Chapter 8: Conclusion

The journey through Alzheimer's disease is a challenging one, marked by progressive cognitive decline and significant emotional and physical demands on patients and their caregivers. However, the development of treatments like Kisunla (donanemab-azbt) offers new hope and possibilities for managing this complex condition. As we reflect on the various aspects of Kisunla and its role in Alzheimer's care, it is essential to consider the broader implications for patients, caregivers, and the future of Alzheimer's research and treatment.

Kisunla represents a significant advancement in the treatment of early symptomatic Alzheimer's disease. By targeting amyloid plaques in the brain, Kisunla addresses one of the key pathological features of the disease. The clinical trials and research supporting Kisunla have demonstrated its potential to reduce amyloid plaque levels, slow cognitive decline, and improve patient outcomes. These findings underscore the importance of early intervention and the potential benefits of targeting the underlying mechanisms of Alzheimer's disease.

The administration and dosage of Kisunla are carefully designed to maximize its therapeutic effects while minimizing potential risks. The intravenous infusion method ensures that the drug reaches the brain in sufficient quantities, and the regular monitoring protocols help detect and manage any adverse reactions. The involvement of healthcare providers, caregivers, and patients in the treatment process is crucial for ensuring safety and efficacy. Effective communication, education, and support are key components of successful treatment with Kisunla.

Understanding the potential side effects of Kisunla is essential for making informed decisions about treatment. While the prospect of side effects can be daunting, it is important to recognize that Kisunla offers significant benefits for individuals with early symptomatic Alzheimer's disease. By targeting amyloid plaques, Kisunla has the potential to slow cognitive decline and improve the quality of life for patients. With careful monitoring and management, the risks associated with Kisunla can be minimized, allowing patients to experience the full therapeutic potential of this groundbreaking treatment.

Patient considerations for Kisunla treatment encompass a range of factors, including eligibility criteria, precautions, contraindications, and genetic risk factors. A thorough evaluation of these factors ensures that patients receive the most appropriate care and that potential risks are minimized. The involvement of caregivers and patient education are also critical components of the treatment process, empowering patients and their families to navigate the challenges of Alzheimer's disease with confidence and support.

Living with Alzheimer's disease requires a multifaceted approach that addresses the physical, cognitive, emotional, and social aspects of the disease. By creating a supportive environment, engaging in regular physical and mental activities, maintaining a balanced diet, managing medications, ensuring safety, and planning for legal and financial matters, individuals with Alzheimer's can improve their quality of life. Support systems, including caregiver support and community resources, play a vital role in helping individuals and families navigate the challenges of the disease. Through education and awareness, we can foster a more understanding and supportive society for those affected by Alzheimer's disease.

The future directions in Alzheimer's research and treatment are characterized by innovation, collaboration, and a commitment to improving the lives of those affected by the disease. Advances in understanding the underlying mechanisms of Alzheimer's, the development of new therapeutic approaches, and the integration of biomarkers and technology are paving the way for more effective and personalized treatments. Lifestyle interventions, gene therapy, and stem cell therapy represent promising avenues for future research. Collaborative efforts and comprehensive support for caregivers are essential for addressing the multifaceted challenges of Alzheimer's disease. As we continue to explore these future directions, there is hope that we will move closer to a world where Alzheimer's disease can be effectively prevented, managed, and ultimately cured.

In conclusion, Kisunla offers a promising new approach to the treatment of early symptomatic Alzheimer's disease. By targeting amyloid plaques, Kisunla addresses one of the key pathological features of the disease and has the potential to slow cognitive decline and improve patient outcomes. The careful administration and monitoring of Kisunla, combined with a comprehensive approach to patient care, ensure that patients receive the most appropriate and effective treatment. As we look to the future, continued research and innovation will be essential for advancing our understanding of Alzheimer's disease and developing new treatments that can further improve the lives of those affected by this challenging condition. Through collaboration, education, and support, we can work towards a brighter future for individuals with Alzheimer's disease and their families.